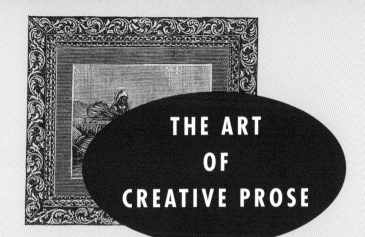

THE ART OF CREATIVE PROSE

PAINTING THE PICTURE

IMAGERY AND DESCRIPTION

VALERIE BODDEN

Creative Education

Published by Creative Education
P.O. Box 227, Mankato, Minnesota 56002
Creative Education is an imprint of The Creative Company

Design by Stephanie Blumenthal
Production by The Design Lab
Art direction by Rita Marshall
Printed in the United States of America

Photographs by 123RF (Christian Musat), Alamy (Danita Delimont), Corbis (Academy of Natural
Sciences of Philadelphia), Getty Images (Ulf Andersen, English School, Hulton Archive, After John
Tenniel, Time Life Pictures/Mansell/Time Life Pictures), The Granger Collection, New York,
iStockphoto (Kasia Biel, Andrew Cribb, Eric Isselée, Peeter Viisimaa), pp. 10–11 Gary Kelley ©2008

Excerpt on pages 16–17 by Upton Sinclair, *The Jungle*.
New York: Penguin Books USA Inc., 1985, pp. 32–33.

Excerpt on pages 24–27 by Dennis Lehane, *Mystic River*.
New York: HarperCollins Publishers Inc., 2001, pp. 3–4.

Library of Congress Cataloging-in-Publication Data

Bodden, Valerie.
Painting the picture: imagery and description / by Valerie Bodden.
p. cm. — (The art of creative prose)
Includes index.
ISBN 978-1-58341-623-5
1. English language—Rhetoric. 2. English language—Style.
3. Creative writing. I. Title. II. Series.

PE1403.B625 2008
808'.042—dc22   2007018964

24689753

WHEN YOU OPEN A BOOK, YOUR EYES ARE MET BY NOTHING MORE THAN WORDS ON A PAGE. Yet, when you read a book, you see more than words—you see the pictures, hear the sounds, and feel the emotions that the words represent. Perhaps this is why so many people turn to creative **prose**—short stories and novels—to temporarily escape their own lives. While you are watching a **fictional** story take shape in your head, it is easy to tune out the gloomy clouds outside your window, the squawk of your sister's clarinet, or your hurt feelings over not being asked to a party. The fictional realm becomes your world, its figures running and dancing in front of your eyes.

B ut how do authors transform mere words—collections of letters—into a vivid world that seems almost as real as your own? Much of the answer to that question lies in description, the words authors use to represent their fictional land and its characters. Although authors may vary greatly in their use of description—some may offer the bare minimum of details about how a place or character looks, while others may use elaborate **similes** and **metaphors**—nearly every author uses description to some extent. Without description, fictional settings lack reality and substance—readers cannot picture them and thus may lose interest in them.

As vital as description is to storytelling, some readers confess that they skip over long sections of description in works of creative prose. While the fault here may lie with lazy readers, it may also lie with authors who either haven't put enough thought into their description or who have focused too much on description at the expense of the rest of the story. Lackluster description that fails to strike readers with fresh images will fall flat, as will long passages of description written for their own sake rather than to reveal something important about the story. But authors who pay careful attention to description will be well-rewarded with readers eager to jump into the black-and-white pages of their stories again and again in order to revisit the colorful **scenes** they depict.

SEEING IS BELIEVING

Although the old saying holds that "a picture is worth a thousand words," the right thousand words (or the right three words, for that matter) can bring a scene to life as vividly as any painting or photograph—maybe even more so, since words allow readers to add their own imagination to the creative process. And imagination is the key to **imagery**, helping readers to see the pictures painted by the words on the page.

As an author, one of the easiest ways to bring readers into a fictional environment is to show them how it looks. After all, most people rely heavily on their sense of sight, so anything that they can see—whether in real life or in their imagination—will seem more real. By sprinkling small sections of imagery throughout your story, you will help readers constantly see—and come to believe in—the world you have created.

Before you begin to try to write sight images, it is helpful to look carefully at your surroundings. Take note of the texture of tree bark, the distance between houses, the color of the sidewalk, the bending of the grass in the wind. If you were going to describe these images, what kinds of words would you use? Now, close your eyes and carefully picture the setting you want to create for your readers. As you write, try to re-create that setting as accurately as possible. But don't include every detail you see—that will likely bore readers and slow the story. Instead, pick out the most important aspects of the scene and try to convey them in a unique way to your readers, helping them to see familiar sights in a new light.

The following excerpt from American author Washington Irving's short story "Rip Van Winkle" (1819), about a man who falls asleep in the Catskill Mountains (spelled "Kaatskill" in the story) and awakens 20 years later, contains an abundance of sight images. What kinds of pictures do you imagine as you read these words?

Whoever has made a voyage up the Hudson must remember the Kaatskill mountains. They are a dismembered branch of the great Appalachian family, and are seen away to the west of the river, swelling up to a noble height, and lording it over the surrounding country. Every change of season, every change of weather, indeed, every hour of the day, produces some change in the magical hues and shapes of these mountains, and they are regarded by all the good wives, far and near, as perfect barometers. When the weather is fair and settled, they are clothed in blue and purple, and print their bold outlines on the clear evening sky; but sometimes, when the rest of the landscape is cloudless, they will gather a hood of gray vapors about their summits, which, in the last rays of the setting sun, will glow and light up like a crown of glory.

At the foot of these fairy mountains, the voyager may have descried the light smoke curling up from a village, whose shingle-roofs gleam among the trees, just where the blue tints of the upland melt away into *the fresh green of the nearer landscape....*

I*n that same village,...there lived, many years since, while the country was yet a province of Great Britain, a simple, good-natured fellow, of the name of Rip Van Winkle....*

In a long ramble...on a fine autumnal day, Rip had unconsciously scrambled to one of the highest parts of the Kaatskill mountains.... Panting and fatigued, he threw himself, late in the afternoon, on a green knoll, covered with mountain herbage, that crowned the brow of a precipice. From an opening between the trees he could overlook all the lower country for many a mile of rich woodland. He saw at a distance the lordly Hudson, far, far below him, moving on its silent but majestic course, with the reflection of a purple cloud, or the sail of a lagging bark [small boat], here and there sleeping on its glassy bosom, and at last losing itself in the blue highlands.

As you read this scene, could you picture the mountains "clothed in blue and purple" or gathering a "hood of gray vapors about their summits"? What did the green knoll look like in your mind? Likely, the images you pictured were different from those pictured by any other reader. Because Irving doesn't say how many mountain peaks there are or how far they stretch or exactly what kind of "mountain herbage" grows on them, we are left to fill in these details for ourselves, which makes us feel almost like co-creators of this fictional reality.

In addition to rather standard sight images such as colors and weather, Irving also introduces fresh imagery into his description, saying that the "blue tints of the upland melt away" and that reflections sleep on the "glassy bosom" of the Hudson River. Have you ever thought of a color melting away or of a river as having a bosom? Such unexpected images catch our attention and lead us to see our surroundings in a new way.

Besides showing us what this scene looks like, Irving's description also helps us get a feel for the land he has created. Carefully chosen phrases such as "magical hues" and "fairy mountains" give us a sense that although the mountain setting looks simple enough, this is no ordinary place—it is, in fact, a magical realm where a man can fall asleep and wake up 20 years later, the circumstances of his life completely changed, but himself the same as always. That's part of the magic of imagery: it can help you create a unique land that doesn't exist anywhere else and that is perfect for telling your specific story. So look around you with an observant eye, then sit down and put your imagination to work sketching a new world with words!

Washington Irving (1783–1859)

ENGAGING THE SENSES

Although the sense of sight is one of our most used senses, it is certainly not the only sense we rely upon. Every day, we use all five of our senses—seeing, hearing, smelling, tasting, and touching. Therefore, a fictional world that doesn't evoke any sense but the sense of sight is likely to seem slightly odd—not to mention less believable—to readers. And, in some cases, such as on a dark night, what your character hears or feels might be even more important than what he sees.

Conveying sensory images in creative prose can be difficult. There are fewer words in the English language to describe our other senses—especially smell and taste—than there are to describe sights. And, people's individual perceptions of different sensory images vary greatly. What sounds loud to you may not seem so loud to your grandfather, whose hearing is beginning to fail; what you think smells like wildflowers might smell like weeds to your friend.

Despite these difficulties, it is important to try to convey sensory images to readers as accurately as possible. Of course, you can tell what something sounds like or smells like or tastes like. Or, you can tell what something does not sound like or smell like or taste like. You can also relate what a specific sound or taste or smell reminds you—or your character—of (perhaps the smell of syrup reminds you of Sunday breakfast). Occasionally, you might even try to employ a technique called synesthesia, in which one sense is described in terms of another—for example, describing what a sound looks like or a color tastes like.

As you read the following excerpt from American writer Upton Sinclair's novel *The Jungle* (1906), about the horrid working conditions in Chicago's meat-packing industry at the turn of the 20th century, take note of the techniques the author uses to call up specific sensory images.

It grew darker all the time, and upon the earth the grass seemed to grow less green. Every minute, as the train sped on, the colours of things became dingier; the fields were grown parched and yellow, the landscape hideous and bare. And along with the thickening smoke they began to notice another circumstance, a strange, pungent odour. They were not sure that it was unpleasant, this odour; some might have called it sickening, but their taste in odours was not developed, and they were only sure that it was curious. Now, sitting in the trolley car, they realized that they were on their way to the home of it—that they had travelled all the way from Lithuania to it. It was now no longer something far off and faint, that you caught in whiffs; you could literally taste it, as well as smell it—you could take hold of it, almost, and examine it at your leisure. They were divided in their opinions about it. It was an elemental odour, raw and crude;

it was rich, almost rancid, sensual and strong. There were some who drank it in as if it were an intoxicant; there were others who put their handkerchiefs to their faces. The new emigrants were still tasting it, lost in wonder, when suddenly the car came to a halt, and the door was flung open, and a voice shouted——'Stockyards!'...

*T*hen the party became aware of another strange thing. This, too, like the odour, was a thing elemental; it was a sound—a sound made up of ten thousand little sounds. You scarcely noticed it at first——it sunk into your consciousness, a vague disturbance, a trouble. It was like the murmuring of the bees in the spring, the whisperings of the forest; it suggested endless activity, the rumblings of a world in motion. It was only by an effort that one could realize that it was made by animals, that it was the distant lowing of ten thousand cattle, the distant grunting of ten thousand swine.*

With this sensory-packed description, Sinclair provides us with our first impression of the Chicago stockyards—and it is an impression that evokes the reality of the stockyards more fully than a purely sight-focused description could. Although Sinclair renders the smell of the stockyards as specifically as possible—it is "pungent," "elemental," "raw," "crude," "rich," "rancid," "sensual," and "strong"—he cannot tell us exactly what it smells like, nor whether it is pleasant or unpleasant. His characters, in fact, are divided over this very issue, reinforcing the fact that different people find different smells attractive or repulsive. How did you feel about the smell as you read the description? Is it something you would like to inhale? What about taste? Notice that Sinclair says that the characters could taste the smell—which is not unusual, since these two senses are often linked.

Upton Sinclair (1878–1968)

The sound of the stockyard is also described in a unique way. It is obviously a complex sound, seeming to be "made up of ten thousand little sounds," which, as we quickly find out, it is. As we read Sinclair's description of what the sound is like—"the murmuring of the bees" or "the whisperings of the forest"—we can almost see the story's characters trying to put their finger on exactly what they are hearing, and we too try to figure it out.

In just this short excerpt, Sinclair has engaged four of our five senses; the only one neglected is touch. Of course, not every description needs to involve so many senses—in fact, some senses may not be appropriate in some scenes, as our sense of taste isn't usually active unless we are eating, and we may not notice the smell of something unless it is particularly strong—but including the perceptions of more than one sensory organ will help to make your scenes more realistic and memorable. So close your eyes and observe the world through your other senses—then make your readers do the same.

IT'S IN THE WORDS

A writer's most important tools are words— not just any words, but the right ones. When you write, you should think carefully about each word you choose. In writing description, some beginning writers are tempted to throw in as many adjectives (words that describe **nouns**) and adverbs (words that describe **verbs**) as possible, thinking that these are "descriptive" words. While adjectives and adverbs certainly can be descriptive, sometimes they are less effective than a strong noun or verb that can stand on its own. For example, rather than saying that a light "shone brightly," you could say that it "glinted," "glimmered," "glared," "twinkled," "glittered," or "gleamed." Any of these verbs would likely convey a more specific picture than the verb-adverb combination of "shone brightly." In addition, each of these specific, strong verbs would bring its own **connotation** to the work. A light that glints or glares may suggest something sinister or unpleasant, while one than "glitters" or "twinkles" might suggest warmth and safety.

Of course, sometimes adjectives and adverbs are needed to more fully convey your meaning. In such cases, **modifiers** should be chosen just as carefully as nouns and verbs. Rather than describing a character's hair as simply "blond," you might describe it as "honey-colored," "bleached," or "golden" to give readers a more precise picture.

As you write your descriptions, it is also important to think about what specific details to include. For example, rather than describing a character's scent, you could include the detail that she wears Chanel No. 5 perfume, for which she pays $114.99 a bottle—but only if it's relevant to the story. Too many specific details can bog a story down and actually make it harder to imagine, but the right details at the right time can help bring a story more fully to life. Notice how American author Dennis Lehane integrates details, modifiers, and carefully chosen nouns and verbs into his descriptions in this excerpt from *Mystic River* (2001), a novel about three childhood friends who find themselves connected by a murder as adults.

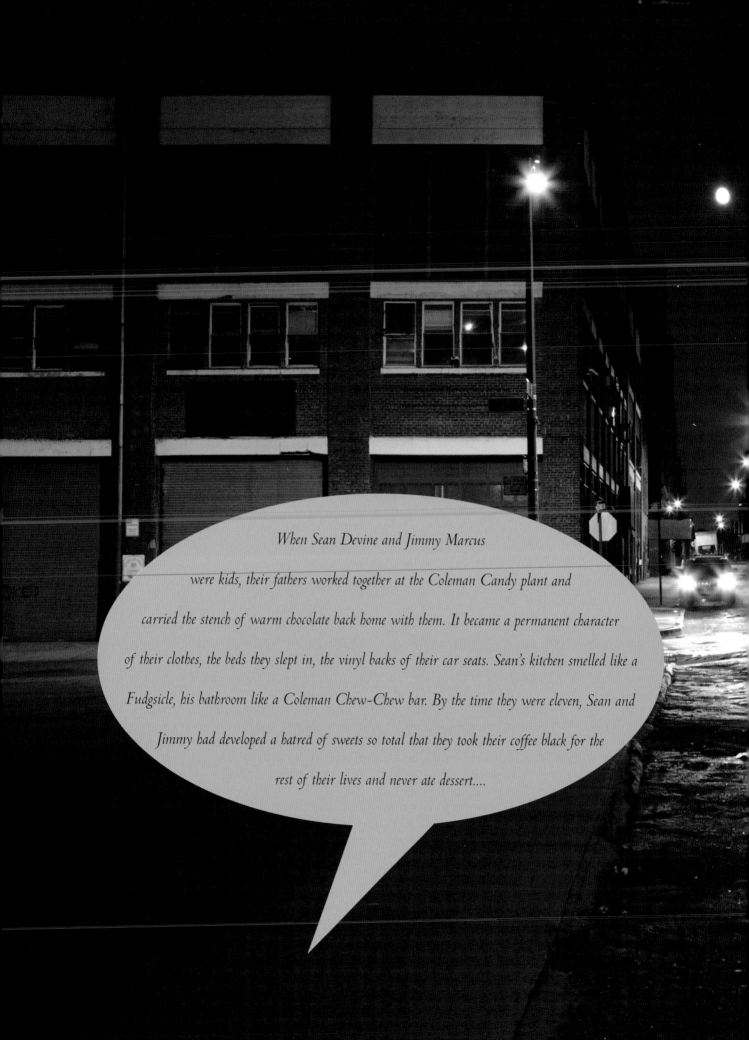

When Sean Devine and Jimmy Marcus

were kids, their fathers worked together at the Coleman Candy plant and

carried the stench of warm chocolate back home with them. It became a permanent character

of their clothes, the beds they slept in, the vinyl backs of their car seats. Sean's kitchen smelled like a

Fudgsicle, his bathroom like a Coleman Chew-Chew bar. By the time they were eleven, Sean and

Jimmy had developed a hatred of sweets so total that they took their coffee black for the

rest of their lives and never ate dessert....

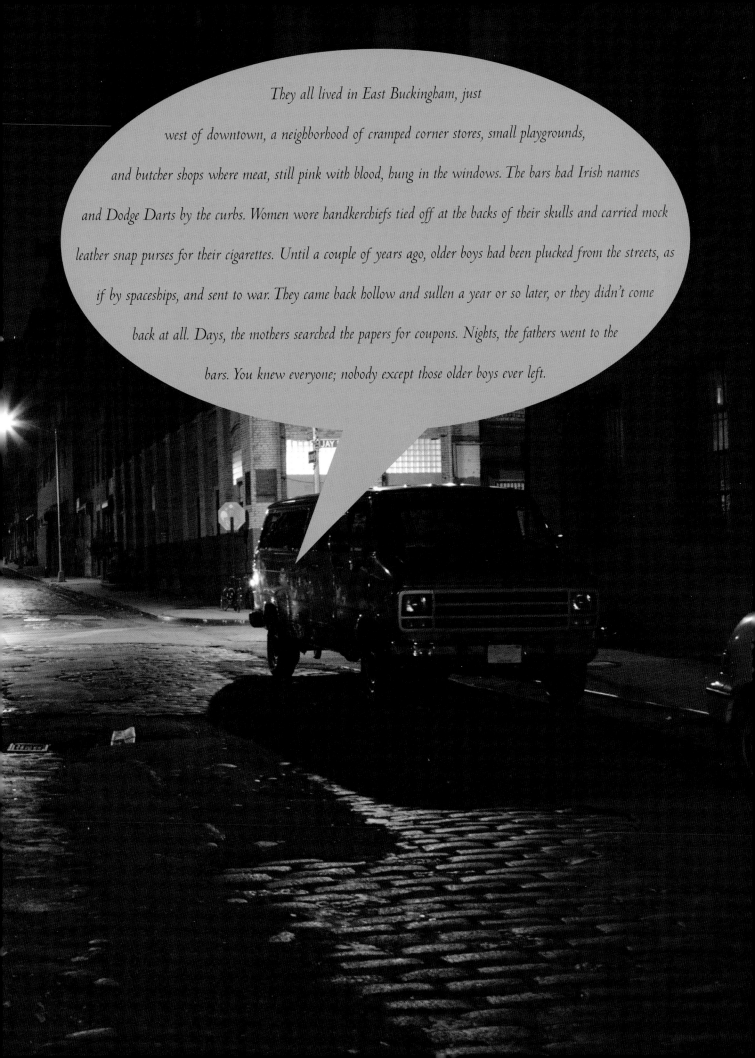

They all lived in East Buckingham, just west of downtown, a neighborhood of cramped corner stores, small playgrounds, and butcher shops where meat, still pink with blood, hung in the windows. The bars had Irish names and Dodge Darts by the curbs. Women wore handkerchiefs tied off at the backs of their skulls and carried mock leather snap purses for their cigarettes. Until a couple of years ago, older boys had been plucked from the streets, as if by spaceships, and sent to war. They came back hollow and sullen a year or so later, or they didn't come back at all. Days, the mothers searched the papers for coupons. Nights, the fathers went to the bars. You knew everyone; nobody except those older boys ever left.

Jimmy and Dave came from the Flats, down by the Penitentiary Channel on the south side of Buckingham Avenue. It was only twelve blocks from Sean's street, but the Devines were north of the Ave., part of the Point, and the Point and Flats didn't mix much.

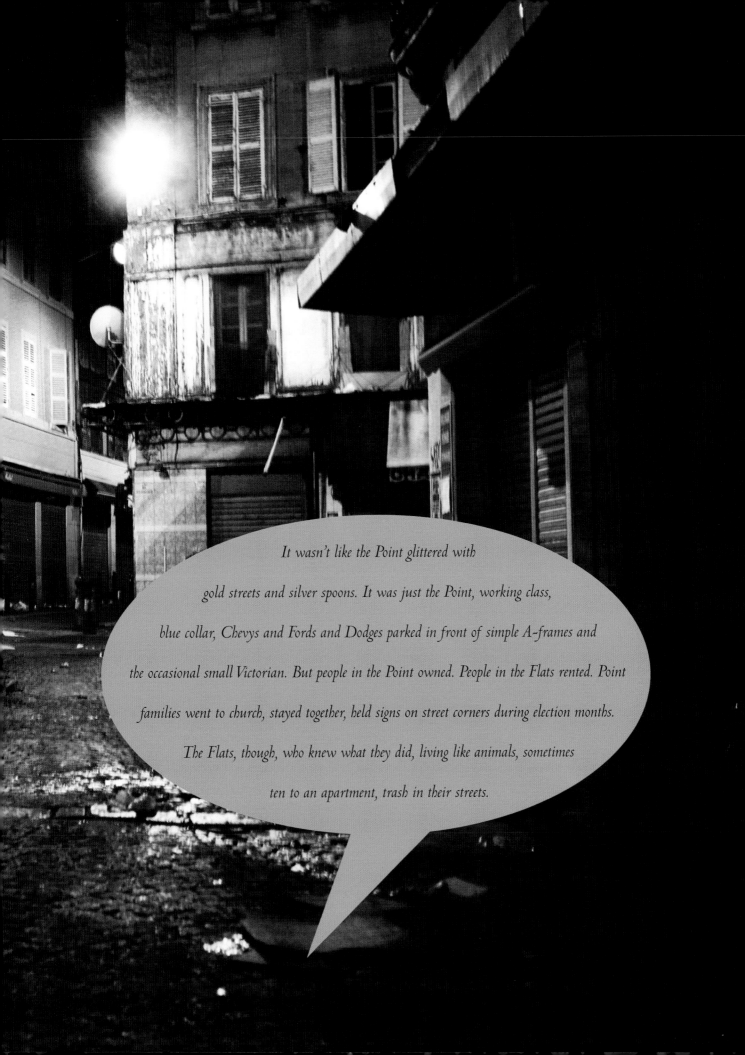

It wasn't like the Point glittered with gold streets and silver spoons. It was just the Point, working class, blue collar, Chevys and Fords and Dodges parked in front of simple A-frames and the occasional small Victorian. But people in the Point owned. People in the Flats rented. Point families went to church, stayed together, held signs on street corners during election months. The Flats, though, who knew what they did, living like animals, sometimes ten to an apartment, trash in their streets.

As we read this excerpt, we can see that Lehane has chosen his words carefully and deliberately. Rather than relying on an overabundance of adjectives and adverbs, Lehane uses strong nouns and verbs to help us imagine the scene. The boys' fathers didn't carry the "sweet smell," but the "stench" of chocolate home from work with them. The older boys didn't "go unwillingly to war," they were "plucked from the streets." The mothers didn't simply "carefully clip" coupons, they "searched" the papers for them.

At the same time, Lehane has also skillfully woven well-chosen modifiers into his description to help us see the town more clearly. Thus, the town doesn't have just stores, but "cramped corner stores," and not just playgrounds, but "small playgrounds." Without these adjectives and adverbs, this town could be any town, with any stores and any playgrounds, but with them, it becomes a specific town with particular kinds of stores and playgrounds.

Another way that Lehane paints a unique scene rather than a generic one is by using a few precise details. Rather than simply saying that Sean's house smelled like the chocolate treats his father manufactured, Lehane helps us smell specific kinds of chocolate treats: Fudgsicles and Coleman Chew-Chew bars. Other details—including street names, vehicle types, and architectural styles— also help us picture a particular setting rather than a vague one. Although he uses a number of such precise details, Lehane also knows where to stop. Had he included the names of all of the stores and bars in the town or a list of the other brand-name products that characterize people from the neighborhoods of the Point or the Flats, he may have found readers tuning out or skipping over his description. So think carefully about every word you write; your story—and your readers' interest—depends on it.

Dennis Lehane (1966–)

When you look at the world around you, you see what is literally there. You see an apple as an apple, a pencil as a pencil, a phone as a phone. But sometimes, when you're writing a description, telling readers what you literally see isn't enough. Sometimes, in order to help readers think about things in new ways, you may choose to describe them **figuratively**. Unlike literal language, figurative language implies something other than what it says. The most common figures of speech—similes and metaphors—describe one thing by comparing it to another.

In a simile, the author tells readers what something "is like" in order to help them better imagine it. Therefore, rather than saying that a tornado was destructive, a simile might say that it "was like a rampaging bear." In place of "like," similes can also use the word "as": "his hands were as scaly as snakeskin." While new, fresh similes can help readers picture two unlike things in a new way, overused similes—called **clichés**—can bore readers. Clichés such as "red like a rose" or "as quiet as a mouse" have been used so many times that they mean little more than the words "red" or "quiet" do on their own.

Unlike a simile, a metaphor doesn't rely on "like" or "as" but transfers the qualities of one object to another by saying that the first object *is* the second. For example, rather than saying that a tornado is "like a rampaging bear" or his hands are "as scaly as snakeskin," a metaphor would say that the tornado *is* a rampaging bear or his hands *are* snakeskin. Such images require a bit more work on the part of the readers' imagination, but they can also leave a stronger impression, forcing readers to connect two unlike objects. Of course, the two objects in a metaphor probably shouldn't be so unlike that readers have a hard time picturing one as the other (for example, you probably wouldn't say that a house is a river unless you have a very specific image in mind and can effectively convey that image to your readers). You should also be careful not to mix metaphors, starting with one image and then switching to another (for example, first calling a person a "sly fox" and then later referring to him as a "gentle dove").

Used correctly, similes and metaphors can add depth and meaning to your writing. Notice how American author Sarah Orne Jewett employs figurative language to help evoke the beauty of the following scene from "A White Heron" (1886), a short story about a young girl's search for an elusive white heron.

There was the huge tree asleep yet in the paling moonlight, and small and silly Sylvia began with utmost bravery to mount to the top of it, with tingling, eager blood coursing the channels of her whole frame, with her bare feet and fingers, that pinched and held like bird's claws to the monstrous ladder reaching up, up, almost to the sky itself....

The tree seemed to lengthen itself out as she went up, and to reach farther and farther upward. It was like a great main-mast to the voyaging earth; it must truly have been amazed that morning through all its ponderous frame as it felt this determined spark of human spirit wending its way from higher branch to branch. Who knows how steadily the least twigs held themselves to advantage this light, weak creature on her way! The old pine must have loved his new dependent....

Sylvia's face was like a pale star, if one had seen it from the ground, when the last thorny bough was past, and she stood trembling and tired but wholly triumphant, high in the tree-top. Yes, there was the sea with the dawning sun making a golden dazzle over it, and toward that glorious east flew two hawks with slow-moving pinions.... Their gray feathers were as soft as moths....

Where was the white heron's nest in the sea of green branches...? Now look down again, Sylvia, where the green marsh is set among the shining birches and dark hemlocks; there where you saw the white heron once you will see him again; look, look! a white spot of him like a single floating feather comes up from the dead hemlock and grows larger....

She knows his secret now, the wild, light slender bird that floats and wavers, and goes back like an arrow presently to his home in the green world beneath.

I n just this short excerpt, Jewett has provided a number of similes that help us picture the scene more clearly. These figures of speech help us to see Sylvia's fingers and feet grasping the tree "like bird's claws," showing us that she is at home in nature. Later, Sylvia's face is "like a pale star," illustrating again that she is part of the natural world. Other similes describe the tree, the hawks, and the heron. Can you identify them? What do you think these similes add to the description?

Sarah Orne Jewett (1849–1909)

Although Jewett doesn't use as many metaphors as similes, these figures of speech are also present: the tree is a "monstrous ladder," and the forest's green branches are a "sea." In addition to these metaphors, Jewett also makes use of another type of metaphor called personification, in which an inanimate object is referred to as if it were a person. In this excerpt, Jewett personifies the tree, saying that he was still sleeping, that he was amazed, and that his twigs held themselves so as to help Sylvia climb. Although the tree can't really do these things, personifying it helps us to see this inanimate object in a new way—almost as a helpful friend on Sylvia's climb. Inventive figures of speech can be as refreshing as a midsummer's twilight swim—or they can even *be* a twilight swim—so experiment with similes and metaphors until you find the right one to reveal your scene in a fresh way.

SHOWING THE PICTURE

I t's easy to write "Sally was in love" or "Bill was lonely." But such statements aren't exciting—to write or to read. That's because it *tells* readers something rather than *showing* it to them. Telling readers that a character was in love doesn't give them a picture of what being in love was like for that particular character. Did she see everything as looking cheerful even on a rainy day? Did she pick at her food without really tasting it? Did she write her name next to his over and over again in her notebook?

Concrete images can help give readers a clear understanding of emotions and other **abstract** ideas. Because everyone's experiences of concepts such as love, loneliness, beauty, and patriotism differ, readers need specific images to help them know what these abstractions mean to your character and your story. Such images also help bring a story to life more vividly than telling does. For

example, it's much more vivid to picture a character wiping her sweaty palms on her pants for the twelfth time than it is to say that she was nervous. As long as you've shown the right sensory images, readers will be able to figure out your character's feelings or state of mind on their own—and they might even be reminded of a time they felt the same way, which can help them identify more closely with your story.

Of course, as with every "rule" in writing, the adage "Show, don't tell" can—and sometimes should—be broken. While too much telling can leave a story lifeless, too much showing can take over a story, burying the important details underneath mountains of less important information. Therefore, a balance of showing and telling is usually called for. In the following excerpt from the novel *White Fang* (1906) by American author Jack London, take note of the combination of showing and telling. What abstract idea or emotion do you think this excerpt illustrates?

Dark spruce forest frowned on either side [of] the frozen waterway. The trees had been stripped by a recent wind of their white covering of frost, and they seemed to lean toward each other, black and ominous, in the fading light. A vast silence reigned over the land. The land itself was a desolation, lifeless, without movement, so lone and cold that the spirit of it was not even that of sadness. There was a hint in it of laughter, but of a laughter more terrible than any sadness—a laughter that was mirthless as the smile of the Sphinx, a laughter cold as the frost and partaking of the grimness of infallibility. It was the masterful and incommunicable wisdom of eternity laughing at the futility of life and the effort of life. It was the Wild, the savage, frozen-hearted Northland Wild.

But there was life, abroad in the land and defiant. Down the frozen waterway toiled a string of wolfish dogs.... Leather harness was on the dogs, and leather traces attached them to a sled which dragged *along behind.... On the sled, securely lashed, was a long and narrow oblong box. There were other things on the sled—blankets, an axe, and a coffeepot and frying pan; but prominent, occupying most of the space, was the long and narrow oblong box.*

In advance of the dogs, on wide snowshoes, toiled a man. At the rear of the sled toiled a second man. On the sled, in the box, lay a third man whose toil was over—a man whom the Wild had conquered and beaten down until he would never move nor struggle again. It is not the way of the Wild to like movement. Life is an offense to it, for life is movement; and the Wild aims always to destroy movement. It freezes the water to prevent it running to the sea; it drives the sap out of trees till they are frozen to their mighty hearts; and most ferociously and terribly of all does the Wild harry [attack] and crush into submission, man.

As we read this excerpt, we not only see the scene that London is creating; we also feel the emotions that the scene conveys. The cold, empty, harsh picture he presents makes us feel lonely and perhaps small and powerless against the forces of nature. Rather than *telling* us that the Northland Wild is a lonely, fearsome place, though, London *shows* us. He shows us the frowning forest, the stripped trees, the silence, and—perhaps most powerful of all—the coffin on the sled. All of these images combine to make us feel the overwhelming emptiness of the landscape and the loneliness of struggling to survive within it.

Although London uses a number of concrete images to evoke the feeling of this place, he doesn't rely solely on showing us the scene. He also tells us that the wilderness is "lone" and "a desolation," and that it has a spirit not of sadness, but of mirthless laughter at the futility of life. By themselves, these abstract ideas would likely be hard to understand, but in combination with the excerpt's concrete images, they help us get an even deeper feel for this land that seeks to bring an end to all life and movement.

Jack London (1876–1916)

As you show your readers the realm your characters inhabit, you will draw them into it—and into your story. When readers can see, hear, taste, feel, smell, and touch your setting, they will believe it is as real as the one in which they live. And they will be delighted every time they come across a phrase that helps them see your story's surroundings—as well as their own—in a new way. So explore every nook and cranny of the world in your imagination, then sit down and draw it for your readers, not with pictures but with words. The results might just be more stunning than any picture could be!

The first step to writing good descriptions is to carefully observe your surroundings. The second step is to practice. The exercises below will help you do both and set you on your way to creating vivid worlds out of words.

OPEN YOUR EYES Go to one of your favorite places. It could be your bedroom, the library, a store, or a park. Spend some time just looking around. Observe not only objects, but also colors, textures, sizes, shapes, and shadows. Now leave the place. Wait an hour or so and then sit down and try to write a scene that recreates the place using only sight images. If you can't remember exactly how something looked, don't settle for a vague image, make something up (after all, this is fiction). When you're done, go back to the place you observed and compare your description to what's really there. Are there any images that are more vivid in real life than in your description? If so, how could you improve your writing?

CHARTING THE SENSES Make a chart with 6 columns and 11 rows. Label the columns "object," "sight," "sound," "smell," "taste," and "touch." Under the object column, write in 10 nouns, such as "bedroom," "apple," and "rain." Now, try to fill in your chart with a specific sight, sound, smell, taste, and touch to describe each object. For example, in the "bedroom" row, you might fill in "red juice stain on the floor" under the sight column and "musty baseball uniform" under the smell column. When you've completed your chart, decide which object you've come up with the most original sensory images for and write a short description of that object using at least three of the five senses.

LOOKING AT LANGUAGE Pull out one of your favorite novels or short stories and open to a page that seems to feature more description than dialogue. Read through the page, making a list of all of the verbs, nouns, adjectives, and adverbs. When you're done, analyze your list. Does the author seem to rely mainly on strong verbs and nouns, or does he or she use a lot of adjectives and adverbs? Do you think some of the story's modifiers could be cut? What would be the result—a stronger or weaker description? Overall, do you think the author's word choices help the story, or could different words have strengthened the prose?

STRIVE FOR ORIGINALITY Clichés are such a huge part of our everyday vocabulary that we sometimes use them without even realizing it. Often, the first simile you come up with will not be the most original, but after a few rewrites, you might find yourself with a fresh image. Try writing at least five similes for each of the following phrases, then decide which, if any, are clichés, and which are original and fresh: "as soft as," "green like," "salty like," "as smelly as," "as loud as." When you're done, try rewriting your fresh similes as metaphors. Think about which descriptions work better as similes and which work better as metaphors.

SHOW, DON'T TELL It's easy to fall into the habit of telling everything and showing nothing. In order to practice what it feels like to show a scene, try to write a description in which you show an emotion or abstract idea without ever naming that emotion or idea. For example, if you chose "beautiful," you would write a scene that describes something beautiful without ever calling it beautiful. When you are done, give your description to a couple of friends or family members to read. Have them try to figure out what idea or emotion you are trying to convey in the scene. If they figure it out, you've done your job of showing. If they don't, you may need to rework your description until the emotion or idea becomes clear.

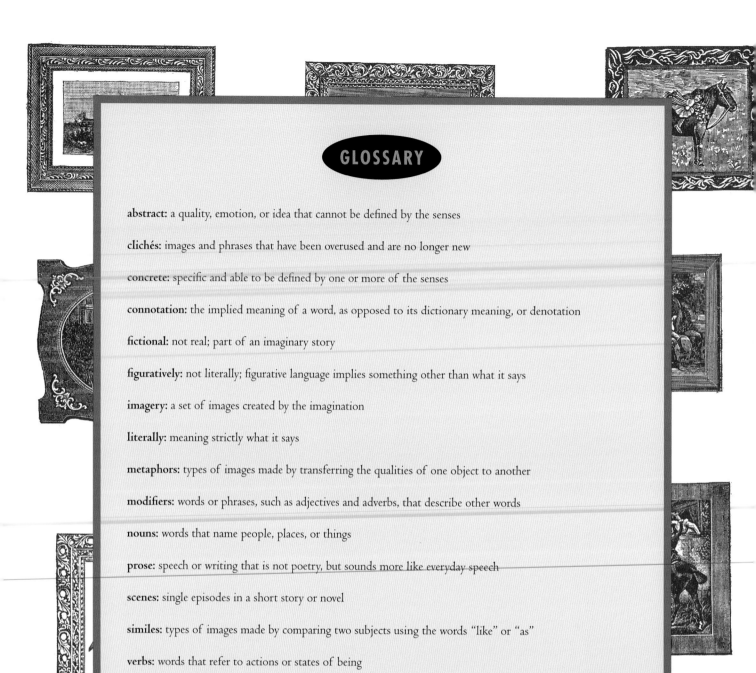

GLOSSARY

abstract: a quality, emotion, or idea that cannot be defined by the senses

clichés: images and phrases that have been overused and are no longer new

concrete: specific and able to be defined by one or more of the senses

connotation: the implied meaning of a word, as opposed to its dictionary meaning, or denotation

fictional: not real; part of an imaginary story

figuratively: not literally; figurative language implies something other than what it says

imagery: a set of images created by the imagination

literally: meaning strictly what it says

metaphors: types of images made by transferring the qualities of one object to another

modifiers: words or phrases, such as adjectives and adverbs, that describe other words

nouns: words that name people, places, or things

prose: speech or writing that is not poetry, but sounds more like everyday speech

scenes: single episodes in a short story or novel

similes: types of images made by comparing two subjects using the words "like" or "as"

verbs: words that refer to actions or states of being

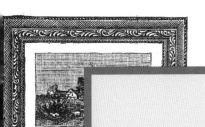

BIBLIOGRAPHY

Bickham, Jack. *Setting*. Cincinnati, Ohio: Writer's Digest Books, 1994.

Conrad, Barnaby. *The Complete Guide to Writing Fiction*. Cincinnati, Ohio: Writer's Digest Books, 1990.

Fandel, Jennifer. *Metaphors, Similes, and Other Word Pictures*. Mankato, Minn.: Creative Education, 2006.

Lyon, Elizabeth. *A Writer's Guide to Fiction*. New York: Perigee, 2004.

McClanahan, Rebecca. *Word Painting: A Guide to Writing More Descriptively*. Cincinnati, Ohio: Writer's Digest Books, 1999.

Rubie, Peter. *The Elements of Storytelling*. New York: John Wiley & Sons, 1996.

Sorenson, Sharon. *How to Write Short Stories*. New York: Macmillan, 1998.

Wood, Monica. *Description*. Cincinnati, Ohio: Writer's Digest Books, 1995.

FURTHER READING

Irving, Washington. *The Complete Tales of Washington Irving*. Edited by Charles Neider. New York: Da Capo Press, 1998.

Jewett, Sarah Orne. *Novels and Stories*. New York: Penguin Putnam, 1994.

Lehane, Dennis. *Mystic River*. New York: William Morrow, 2001.

London, Jack. *The Call of the Wild and White Fang*. New York: Bantam Books, 1981.

Sinclair, Upton. *The Jungle*. New York: Penguin Books, 1985.

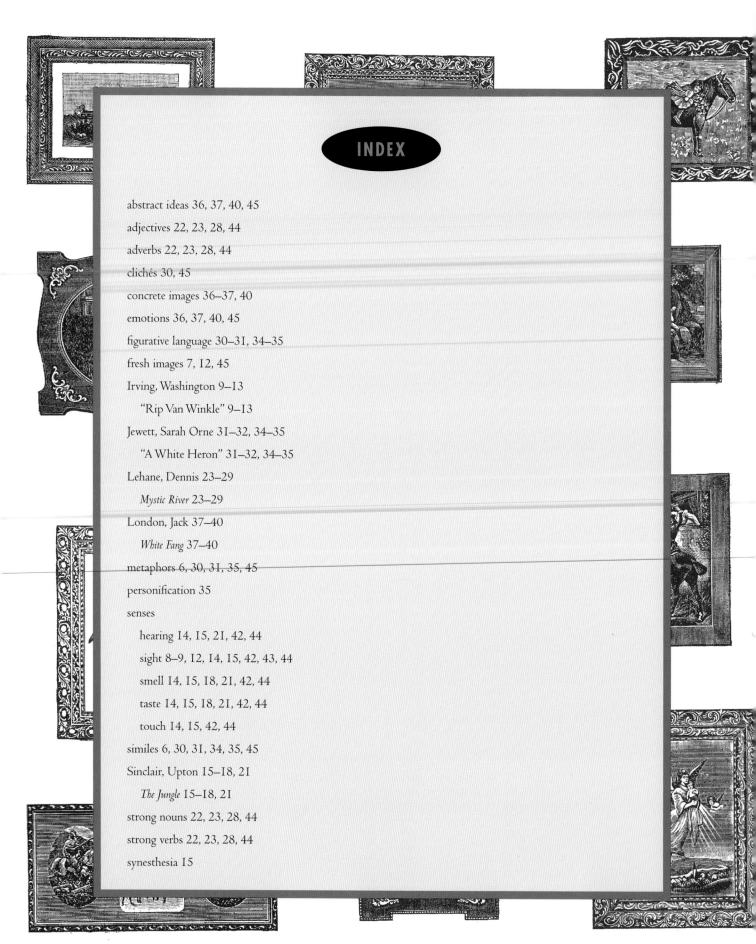

INDEX